GATE HAPPY

About Leaving Prison

Simeon Sturney

Sarah GRACE PUBLISHING
Dyslexic Friendly

First published 2023 by Sarah Grace Publishing
an imprint of Malcolm Down Publishing ltd.
www.sarahgracepublishing.co.uk

27 26 25 24 23   7 6 5 4 3 2 1

British Library Cataloguing in Publication Data
A catalogue record for this book is available from the British Library.

ISBN 978-1-915046-57-4

Cover design by Angela Selfe

Art direction by Sarah Grace

Printed in the UK

Dedication

This book is dedicated to everyone working alongside
people leaving prison – you are unsung heroes!

Introduction

This booklet is for:

- Frontline staff with His Majesty's Prison and Probation Service (HMPPS),
- Those in a support role for HMPPS,
- Through The Gate services that work alongside offenders coming out of prison, and
- Third Sector agencies involved in supporting ex-offenders, and
- People who want to learn more, debate, reflect, and even pray.

The focus is on supporting prisoners being released from the female estate but also relevant to the male estate.

The booklet is an introduction to the mixed-up, confusing world of emotions and experiences women often go through when being released from prison. 'One of the most vivid yet psychologically illuminating pieces of prison slang is "Gate fever", defined by *The Concise Dictionary of Crime and Justice* as "the emotional feeling experienced by prison inmates scheduled for release. Gate fever includes anxiety about where they will live, what they will do to earn a living, and whether they will be able to refrain from engaging in crime"' (The Butler Trust, 2022).

The booklet is a useful tool for those working directly with prisoners at the point of their release as well as giving an overview of some of the issues women face, which could be of value to staff beginning their career, as part of their induction. It assists the reader in understanding some of the emotions many prison leavers face. It is written in the form of editorial articles containing observations I have garnered as a Through The Gate prison chaplain, having listened to and journeyed with hundreds of women over many years. The articles can be read separately or together. They tell an often-untold story of the issues, realities and emotions women face at the point of their release, using various anecdotes. The booklet is not a comprehensive guide to the release process but is insightful and thought provoking.

You are invited to pick a title that takes your eye and reflect upon it. The booklet doesn't need to be read from cover to cover, but rather from interest to interest. Each chapter is a 'stand-alone' article, written in an editorial style. At the end of every article is a reflection section with a personal question, asking how you would respond to something raised in the piece. You may want to discuss this with others.

Permission is given for up to three articles to be reproduced without seeking the publisher's permission if they are attributed to the author and book – *Gate Happy*.

EDITORIAL SERIES: to highlight the issues female prisoners face at the exact point of their release.

Readership: customers (a) prison and probation staff, stakeholders with oversight for prison receptions, budgeting and policy influencers, providers of Through The Gate services; (b) interested parties involved with social justice and prison ministry (NGOs, etc.).

Aim: to encourage educated support at the immediate point of release – both in the prison reception area and as they walk through the main gate back into the community.

Happy to

Happy to be free from iron bars,

Happy to walk out through the prison gate,

Happy to be met by a partner,

Happy to walk away from rules,

Happy to do 'one's thing',

Happy to enjoy the drug of choice,

Happy to choose how to pay,

Happy to take the risk,

Happy to suffer the blow, kick, or punch,

Happy to run and hide,

Happy to be 'out of it',

Happy to do it all again,

Happy to do it all again,

Happy to do it all again,

Happy to be arrested for nicking,

Happy to be back in prison.

Simeon Sturney

Articles Index

EDITORIAL: to highlight the importance of a simple conversation with women as they travel to their next destination.

Aim: to encourage ordinary conversation when supporting people at the point of release – especially for women heading back into the community.

EDITORIAL: to highlight the spirit of resilience some released prisoners have.

Aim: to encourage readers to understand the hope some ex-prisoners hold on to.

EDITORIAL: to highlight the complexities of housing people who have been homeless.

Aim: to encourage honest conversations with clear expectations regarding housing.

EDITORIAL: to highlight the focus some people have when they are released from prison.

Aim: to raise awareness of the 'all-consuming' focus addiction has on some people.

EDITORIAL: to highlight the importance of a non-judgemental attitude when supporting people released from prison.

Aim: to acknowledge people can resettle positively from prison.

10. The 'F' word 51

11. 'Oh my God' 55

12. Where are they now? 59

ARTICLES

1

The Bag Carrier

EDITORIAL: to introduce the role of Through The Gate support and its importance.

Aim: to encourage extra support at the immediate point of release – especially within the prison reception/discharge area.

'What do you do, sir?'

Before I have time to answer, a fan of mine pipes up, 'He carries ya bags. He's alright, he is.'

With that ringing endorsement I go on to explain to the first woman exactly what I do. The three of us are sat in a 'holding cell', within the reception area of western Europe's largest women's prison. The two women alongside me are going through the exit process on the day of their release. I share how I meet the women moments prior to their release and am on hand to answer any questions and give any support that may be required. I let them know that there is a free hot drink in the visitors' centre waiting for them and, if they need me, I can walk with them to the train station. It is during this activity that I assist in carrying bags.

'You're alright, love,' the first woman states confidently. 'I got someone meeting me,' she declares with a big smile and then, after rummaging in the property she has just been given, goes on to spray perfume on herself and anything else that moves! I'm thinking it's probably not her mother waiting outside. I've never been to a brothel and perhaps I don't need to. I'm told the holding cell, with women having changed into clothing they are not allowed to wear in prison, creates the same vibe. I'm a chaplain, specialising in Through The Gate support, so what do I know? However, on one occasion, when walking to the station with a couple of newly released women, one of them asked if there was anything she could do for me – they had just been talking about how they fund their drug habit as 'working girls'. The other woman chastised her, reminding her that I'm a 'man of God'. 'Yeah, but it wouldn't be the first time!' she retorted. I just looked over my glasses, no need to comment.

The truth is I know more than many of my clerical friends. I hear and see things that are extremely challenging, especially for the women being released. I hear stories of childhood neglect and abuse. Many leave still craving their drug of choice, going back into the same routine that brought them into prison. Over half of the fifteen or so women I meet a week are 'frequent flyers' or 'revolving door' women, regulars who have been recalled for non-compliance of their licence conditions or just given short sentences. They have not been in long enough to address their addiction or lifestyle. Most of those who are without accommodation will be advised to go to their probation appointment where they will be given further instruction, often involving the homeless persons' unit at their council, where a bed for the night is often on offer. A significant number each week decide to abort any efforts to comply, some in the belief that there won't be anywhere 'safe' for them. Sadly, in opting out they may be putting themselves at greater risk from sexual, violent and emotional abuse. Their minds are sometimes swayed by others they meet in the reception area, who invite them to join them as they head off to find the 'crack'. Many of the women I come across have lost hope, resigned themselves to a life that leaves them vulnerable. Even though they put on a show of bravado, low self-esteem, depression and anxiety are never too far away.

I have no magic wand, but having journeyed with numerous women over many years, I can be of assistance. One of the most important things I do is listen. I listen with time on my hands, listen with no agenda and no authority, especially once we're in the community. I'm an extra pair of hands, assisting the often-hard-pressed officers in Reception. I can answer simple questions regarding the release procedure or ring a case worker when a query arises. I can be a calming influence in a busy department, a reassuring figure as I offer to walk alongside the bamboozled first-timer — unaware of where she is in the world, both physically and emotionally. Our prison can be many miles away from the woman's home area and she may be unfamiliar with train travel or struggle to read or even speak English. I've even been asked to say a prayer for the woman or two as we wait on the platform, always a little awkward when they get down on their knees — closed eyes, clasped hands and straight in front of my midriff. I quickly move to the side and dispatch a prayer of comfort and hope. I'm even there for the woman whose boyfriend fails to turn up and she is left disappointed, angry and lost.

But my role is unusual. My prison has decided to invest in this extra layer of support. Some prisons would see it as a luxury. However, I maintain that my very presence can dissuade women from teaming up with others in the holding cell, reminding them of what is at stake, or strategically separating people. If I can support a woman to leave prison still holding on to her release plan, encourage her to attend her appointments and let her know that the prison values her so much that they have employed me to be there for her, then there is a good chance she will have positive engagements for the rest of the day. If the first hour goes well, then the second may, and so on. However, if the first hour goes badly, hope for a positive resettlement may dissipate quickly, leading to an early return to prison and all the cost that entails. Investing in someone to transition with the prisoner from the holding cell to the point of their transport and beyond can be a good investment. Much time and many resources are spent formulating release plans and after care, but they are not focused on the holding cell where plans can easily be abandoned. A seamless transition bodes well for a successful resettlement.

Reflection

If you were . . .

. . . being released from prison – who would you like to be there to meet you and who wouldn't you want there?

. . . someone who worked with prisoners just about to be released – what do you think is the most important thing to say to them, moments before they walk out the door?

2

Not like in the movies

EDITORIAL: to highlight some of the issues women face at the point of their release.

Aim: to highlight the need for focused support at the immediate point of release – especially as not everyone who is being met will have a good experience and may benefit from a timely intervention.

She stood there in front of him, her head bowed down as he lambasted her with an aggressive speech. I didn't understand the language, but I got the gist and it wasn't pleasant! Twenty minutes earlier I had been trying to communicate with the woman as we sat in the holding cell of the prison she was just about to be released from. She had enough English to let me know her husband was picking her up and I could tell she was extremely excited, lots of smiles and attention to how she looked. I went ahead, keen to see this romantic greeting. I happened to be standing ten paces behind her husband who was accompanied by a boy in his early teens. I wanted a good view. The main gate rolled back, the woman looked up, immediately spotted her family and the joy on her face was radiant. With a holdall in each hand, she ran towards him, arms opened wide – cue the music and the flowers.

19

But there was no music, no flowers. As she got closer, she began to slow down. The boy took a couple of steps back behind his father and she came to a stop five paces in front of him as he stood upright with his arms folded. 'Hold on,' I thought, 'hasn't he read the script?' Whatever script he was reciting, it wasn't the one she was expecting. Forty-five seconds into his dialogue and I'd had enough. She didn't deserve this, no-one does. I walked past him with a glare and walked up to the woman and wished her all the best for the day, with the biggest smile I could muster. He stopped his verbal abuse and turned around, walked to the car park with his wife and son trailing behind.

Sometimes there are no happy endings. The prison sentence may be over but for some captivity remains. I don't know how it ended that day for the woman delighted to see her family. Perhaps the flowers were in the car, they had a lovely 'welcome home' meal prepared and later a romantic evening watching a favourite movie accompanied by an expensive box of chocolates, but I doubt it. Even if all that was in place, you can't easily recover from the total humiliation shown, served with lashings of vitriol. Things like that anger me, but as a Through The Gate chaplain I have seen plenty more of that unpleasant behaviour and have had to keep my professional 'cool'. I have witnessed plenty of arguments between couples – the woman shouting at the chap who has come to meet her because he didn't send in money or hasn't brought the little gift he promised, or just because he's a 'lazy son of a —' or because he has turned up! 'You said it was over, so what are you doing here?' I've heard that a few times. On one occasion a man turned up in the visitors' centre, obviously shattered from a late night. He said he had come to meet a woman being released and named her. By the time she came out, he was fast asleep with his head on a dining table. I told the woman her friend was in the centre, but when I pointed him out, she said she didn't know him. 'Are you sure? Because he's definitely here to meet you,' I stated. She was genuinely adamant she didn't know him. In one last attempt I shook the table as she peered closer. His creased face emerging from his folded arms was greeted by the woman shouting words to the effect of 'What are you doing here?' She hadn't recognised him at first. He had finished the relationship as he had begun another. He'd moved on. She was shocked and angry. I gave them some space. They needed it and they ended up walking to the station together.

What I have learnt over the years is that just because a woman has someone meeting her, it doesn't mean it's planned, safe and trouble free. I often ask if the woman is being met and if so by whom? If the answer is yes, I will check if she gets on with them. The woman may look at me quizzically, but sometimes they know exactly why I'm asking. Women have disclosed that the bloke isn't great but there isn't anyone else to help her. I have had women ask me to walk with them even though there is a chap in tow, and I know why. At least she'll get on the train before any trouble starts and maybe, if it's crowded, he won't start before they get off and he's cooled down a little. I've learnt it is always good to check if the 'lift' is safe, because not everything or everyone is as they appear. I can be a useful extra layer of support.

Reflection

If you were . . .

. . . the woman being lambasted by someone meeting you from prison – how would you respond?

. . . outside at the same time as someone being met and witnessed bullying – is there anything you would or could do to support the person being bullied?

3

Walking with bottles

EDITORIAL: to highlight the advantages of people escorting newly released prisoners from the gate.

Aim: to encourage non-judgemental attitudes when journeying with people released from prison.

I'm not disclosing a secret need, although I have been known to have a little more of the 'red stuff' than is helpful, and I have been wobbly once or twice. The bottles referred to in the title are those purchased by women from the off-licence, a few minutes after their release from prison. Having turned down my offer to walk with them to the train station, I respond by offering to meet them when they come out of the local shop, this facility being the panacea of all things when it comes to the urgent need to celebrate one's release from the 'establishment'. With my understanding of their need to purchase alcohol, they revise their earlier reticence, especially when a companion of theirs states that 'he's okay and he always waits for me outside'.

With my non-judgemental disposition confirmed, I'm invited to join them on their journey, or should I say to the party? It's not unusual for one of them to ask if there's anything I need from the shop as I offer to wait outside with their bags. I always decline – with a hearty thanks. It isn't just a healthy respect for their choice of shopping that I bring to the gathering, or my muscles. I know I bring comfort and reassurance. As we walk together, the woman with a can in her hand, it isn't uncommon for members of the general public to cross over to the other side for no apparent reason, and because I'm dressed in casual clothes I've often been mistaken as a 'friend' of theirs – you should see the looks some people give us!

The truth is many women 'drink' not to celebrate their freedom but rather to numb their future. They know that in a few hours they will be back on their 'patch', working their charm to purchase the non-prescribed substances they need to either cope with their situation or to buy their way into having a roof over their head for the night. As we walk together, I chat or listen – not as a punter, nor someone with authority or power over them, but just as a man respecting them for who they are, with no strings attached and no hidden agenda. As we walk and talk together, I know I offer a welcome distraction, a friendly smile, and a demeanour that says she's the 'VIP' right now.

Those few moments we are together are priceless not worthless. She knows I'm relating to her as I relate to most people and that brings mutual respect. Her respect affords me the privilege of being told personal information and I'm often asked for my opinion or for advice. It also allows me to challenge her gently regarding some of her plans for the day.

With the occasional clinking of glass on glass coming from a rather flimsy looking plastic bag, we chat about things both light in nature and extremely dark and painful. It's amazing how the same route can take only a few minutes when deep in conversation and yet seemingly twice as long when there's no rapport or friendly chatter. When we've engaged well, I'm ever hopeful the woman will continue that level of engagement at her appointments – should she get there. She may even have rehearsed with me what she is going to say when face to face with her probation officer or how she is going to cope when challenged about previous actions. And there I am, waving her off at the platform hopeful that she will get to her destination safely, when I realise she hadn't taken a sip from her earlier purchases; and, of course, I'm hopeful she discards them before they are opened. It costs nothing to hope and nothing to pray and you may be surprised how many women ask me to pray for them when we're saying goodbye. When that happens, I'm not in charge of the hope anymore, I've passed the responsibility on.

Reflection

If you were . . .

. . . walking away from a prison and aware people were staring at you because they knew you had just been released – how would that make you feel and how would you react?

. . . walking with someone who is being stared at by the public – how would you respond?

4

'Everyone needs a slap now and then'

EDITORIAL: to highlight the abuse women can face upon their release.

Aim: to encourage practical and 'informed' support at the immediate point of release – especially for women facing abuse back in the community.

'No, they don't,' I reply, after being told by a female prisoner that 'everyone needs to be put in their place once in a while'. I agree that people may need to be challenged, but I don't believe 'slapping' is the way to go about it! Yet this is the lived experience of many of the women I walk alongside as they leave the prison. I regularly hear accounts of how a woman has been beaten by her partner, husband or 'punter'. They go on to tell me it's not worth them arguing as it causes more trouble. So, they go out and steal, perform unpleasant 'acts' and sell themselves. I have known women who, moments after their release, have been abused by their partner.

Being beaten by a person who wants to control you as an object, as their possession, is bad – really bad. But when it is justified by God it is evil! Don't get me wrong – I don't believe God is evil, otherwise I really am in the wrong profession. However, I have lost count of the number of times a woman of faith has told me that they must obey their husband because their religion demands it, even if what they are being instructed to do is horrible or illegal. Most mainstream religions do not hold this view. They have a 'get-out' clause regarding safety and well-being. Yet what the woman is told by her husband is that she must submit to him, obey him as he, as the husband, is the head of the family. Christians often quote the Bible and say St Paul says so. Now is not a time for theological debate, but my view is very different, and I believe St Paul is referring to the law at the time. However, Paul says first, 'Submit to one another', something that is often conveniently forgotten. Paul then goes on to remind husbands to love their wives. Again, this statement doesn't appear to register. Instead, the woman in front of me is dutifully reciting her husband's mantra. And what else should she do? If she tries to counter it, she is shut down, disciplined, and even shamed as a disobedient wife. And where can the woman go? Often the only network she knows is other people of a similar faith and possibly in a similar situation. Thankfully there are organisations that have experience in supporting women escaping abuse, but it isn't easy taking the first step.

I have escorted women to the train station who tell me that they haven't told anyone that they were in prison. They don't want to be judged any more than they have been by the court. As a chaplain in the prison, I have been told by women of faith that they don't want their 'congregation' to be informed that they are in prison, as the congregation believe they have gone to family abroad, and the family abroad think they are still in the city working hard to send money back home. They tell me that being in prison would bring much shame upon the family and their family is likely to disown them. This is complicated by the fact that the family is currently looking after the woman's children. If their secret is known, they could lose their children or have strict conditions put upon them when they return. In some cultures, this isn't seen as harsh – it is just how it is.

Escaping abuse, bullying, being manipulated and controlled is everyday life to many women I journey with. A slap in exchange for a roof over their head can seem a 'fair deal'. It isn't to me, but then I don't live with the fear of the alternative, or have to navigate the coercive and controlling behaviour of those around me.

Reflection

If you were . . .

. . . leaving prison and you had a choice between sleeping on the streets or having a roof over your head but having to do things that were extremely unpleasant – what would you choose?

. . . walking with someone who was telling you that where they were going, they knew they were going to be abused – what would you say to them?

5

Keeping it simple

EDITORIAL: to highlight the importance of a simple conversation with women as they travel to their next destination.

Aim: to encourage ordinary conversation when supporting people at the point of release – especially for women heading back into the community.

Sometimes things go according to plan and sometimes they don't. Drama on the walk to the train station with a woman released from prison can make for an interesting story. Less so is a simple trip that goes without a hitch – not much to write about there, almost boring. But, of course, that is what I hope for on most occasions, that the woman gets to the station without any problems and alights the correct train heading in the right direction, or is met at the gate by someone who really cares about them and understands a little of the journey they have been through.

It was one of those boring occasions, the only excitement being a little rain, but no monsoon to boast about. As we walked to the station, the woman was mindful that the volunteer assisting us that day had driven half an hour just to walk with us twenty minutes. As the woman got on the train, she thanked both of us individually and we waved her off. I could see the volunteer was a little deflated. There had been no deep and meaningful conversation, no heartbreak story to show concern about, no heavy bag to carry. It had been uneventful. Then I reminded the volunteer that the woman had known that she had travelled some distance and set off early, just to walk with her in the rain, and all this as someone unpaid to do it. When the woman thanked the volunteer, she knew she was thanking her for the effort she had made, and I know that means a lot to the women being released. Knowing that someone has put themselves out for them – an ex-prisoner, someone often looked down upon by others, someone who is not deemed worthy by many, has had someone go to great lengths to make sure they get out of town safely – that is big to many of the women I journey with. When the volunteer understood the context of the woman's 'thank you', she understood this wasn't a throw-away line, but a statement of real appreciation. The volunteer went home knowing she had made a difference that day.

Some of us, me included, like to be recognised for what we do. A simple 'thank you' is often enough. Some of us may dream of awards, certificates, ceremonies, medals, our name in lights, but few ever admit it. Being recognised can be life- or work-affirming. But for many that dream has long gone. Just being smiled at once a day is an achievement. For some women I walk with, all they want is to be respected for who they are, a person not a number, not some object or 'case'. They would like to be listened to, asked for their opinion, to have a mutually weighted discussion with. It is awesome when a woman gets to the station and with a smile on her face says, 'Thank you for walking with me.' I don't need her to go away assuring me that she has listened to what I've told her, has agreed to never mess up again, and acknowledge how bad she has been. She already knows the 'score', she's living with the results. All some women want is to be treated with dignity, respect, and to be valued for being them.

Reflection

If you were . . .

. . . just released from prison – what ordinary conversation would you look forward to?

. . . walking with someone newly released – what conversation would make you uncomfortable and why?

6

Heroes unwrapped

EDITORIAL: to highlight the spirit of resilience some released prisoners have.

Aim: to encourage readers to understand the hope some ex-prisoners hold on to.

Not all heroes are 'sweet', likeable, lick-able and moreish, although there is a brand of confectionery in the UK that could tempt us to overindulge our 'sweet tooth'. The heroes I'm referring to are those people who, despite the odds being stacked against them, still hope for or dream of a better future and tell themselves it's going to be different 'one day'. Sadly, today may not be that day. My heroes are those women who, as they leave prison, are still holding out for that 'one day' experience. 'That's it, sir, I'm not coming back again,' they insist, as I meet them just prior to their release. 'Again' is the clue that this has not been their first time and, for several, it won't be their last. Unfortunately, there have been a few who have said it and died shortly afterwards – how prophetic their words were. But, for a significant number who deliver this sentence it is spoken in hope rather than with confidence, more 'fingers crossed, touch wood'.

I admire their hope or even their faith that this time it's going to be different. And for some it is! The shock of being detained at His Majesty's pleasure, separated from family and friends, along with a dose of self-reflection, has steered her mind to achieving whatever is required to never return to the establishment. Sometimes we even see some of these women back at the prison – as role models, sharing how it is possible to turn your life around.

However, I specialise in journeying with the 'frequent flyers', 'the revolving door' women. Therefore, I am not surprised when I see women return. What does surprise me is when they say they haven't been in prison for three years, and yet it only seems like last year I was waving them off – I must be getting old! When I hear how well they have done, despite this recent mishap, I am quick to congratulate them for their achievement; especially as previously they would have been back every year, if not twice a year. Some tell me how they have reconnected with family, got a safe place to live and are studying law. Yes, that's quite common. I refrain from suggesting that I thought they were experts already!

When in prison, some women discover the value of study. Others discover benefits from going to the gym, and others discover God or reconnect with their faith. All these things can help when returning to the community and are something they're looking forward to when released – hoping for a fitter mind, body and soul. I always encourage the women to dream their dreams, hold out for hope and 'go for it', if it's positive.

Heroes come in all shapes and sizes and sometimes they are not who you were expecting. Any woman who has experienced homelessness, addiction, abuse and prison, and is still willing to hope for a better life 'one day' is certainly a hero of mine! I'm proud to say I meet several heroes a week, although sadly I wish it were in a different context. 'Fingers crossed, touch wood' and 'on a wing and a prayer', we all hope that the women I journey with stay safe and never return to prison.

Reflection

If you were . . .

. . . in prison – what would you be hoping for upon your release?

. . . hearing someone talk about what they are hoping for – what 'hope' is unrealistic?

7

Housing the homeless

EDITORIAL: to highlight the complexities of housing people who have been homeless.

Aim: to encourage honest conversations with clear expectations regarding housing.

I'm very aware that housing is a major issue for many people leaving prison, as I hear the frustrations of the women I walk alongside nearly every day. Yet housing someone with a chaotic lifestyle is extremely complicated. Holding down a tenancy for someone who is constantly distracted by addiction, surrounded by unhelpful acquaintances, and struggles with keeping to appointments, filling in forms, managing rent monies and keeping to tenancy agreements, can be almost impossible. The expectation that someone homeless and desperate for a roof over their head will of course comply with the obvious regulations, can be misplaced if the person doesn't possess the skills, ability or mindset required. It is like offering someone who is wheelchair-bound an apartment on the seventh floor without there being a lift – however nice the apartment, it is unrealistic to think this is going to be successful. And for someone used to sofa-surfing, coming and going as they please or gaining a bed for the night by 'selling' themselves – is hardly the best training for maintaining a tenancy, no matter how desperate they are.

It has long been accepted that women leaving prison without secure permanent accommodation are vulnerable to exploitation, abuse and the quick return to criminal activities, however well-intentioned they are about turning their lives around. And to that end vast sums of money are put into services and housing projects that offer the haven so desperately sort after. But there are some women who still don't or can't take up the offer and many of these may be referred to as the 'revolving door' prisoners who, even with a room and a key of their own, struggle to settle. Some use the premises as a 'lock-up and leave' storage facility, leaving their few belongings there whilst they still sofa-surf, only returning once or twice a week. I remember a woman telling me she had turned down the offer of accommodation as she said her boyfriend would take up residence and continue his dealing from there. I have met several women whose property has been raided by the police and drugs seized, yet maintain the drugs belonged to their partner. And some partners you just don't want to argue with!

I am not suggesting accommodation shouldn't be made available to chaotic ex-offenders but perhaps a better understanding of the mindset of the individual or their lifestyle needs more scrutiny. There are some fantastic services that provide mentors, befrienders, navigators and 'Through The Gate' workers to assist the person to attend their appointments, fill in forms and encourage good housekeeping. Sadly, there are not enough of these workers. Yet, even with these workers allocated, many women don't take advantage of their services. If a person's mindset can't respond, then whatever resources have been allocated, including finances, could be wasted. Perhaps resources could be directed towards longer interview times between the prisoners and the professionals making the referrals, with stronger emphasis on whether the person truly believes they will be able to commit to everything required of them. Often appointments can be hurried and an implied expectation on the prisoner to agree to comply, almost with the attitude of 'why wouldn't you want to take advantage of this offer?' On numerous occasions, I've walked to the station with women who state they have no intention of attending any appointment, even those they have agreed to. I once asked a woman what she would change about the system supporting people resettling into the community. Her reply wasn't greater housing or more employment opportunities but a request for more time in appointments so they could really explore how she was feeling and the issues she was facing. Maybe inviting people they trust – a family member, good friend or professional from the community – to be part of the discussion regarding their likelihood of compliance could encourage a more-thought-through reply, as the external voice could refer to previous experiences and challenges they've faced. It appears to me that there is a lot of pressure on professionals from targets set to source accommodation, even if the recipient is unlikely to avail themselves of it. Perhaps we need a few more 'honest' conversations.

Reflection

If you were . . .

. . . homeless and being released from prison – what would you agree to, to get a 'safe' roof over your head?

. . . charged with the responsibility of securing accommodation for someone who was presenting as unlikely to manage it appropriately and perhaps not even turn up to collect the keys – how would this make you feel?

8

'On't road'

EDITORIAL: to highlight the focus some people have when they are released from prison.

Aim: to raise awareness of the 'all consuming' focus addiction has on some people.

'On't road' is prison slang for 'on the road', referring to outside prison and often relating to a prisoner's 'home patch'. A prisoner may also refer to knowing someone from 'on't road' or agree when saying goodbye inside, that they will meet up 'on't road'. And 'on't road' may have a different set of rules to the ones many in society follow. A woman familiar with the prison system will know how it works and how to survive, but first-timers may struggle. For the regular who is accustomed to both, she understands the social and cultural rules of prison life, including the prison regulations and discipline of the establishment, as well as the way things operate for her 'on't road'. Going 'underground' and being non-compliant with her post-prison licence conditions, makes her feel a free agent. Sadly, she is likely to be anything but free because the thing that eventually brings her back to prison is the 'all consuming' addiction she has that ties her up and steers her along a well-known path. She is one of prison's 'frequent flyers'.

However, some people are more comfortable with prison life because it's easier. But not because they have all modern conveniences, as some people, often in the media, want to exaggerate. It's easier because they don't have to perform 'tricks' to get a roof over their head, don't have to sleep/rest with one eye open for fear of abuse, don't have to worry about others in the property coming back drunk or 'high' or 'low' or moody or violent. Easy because they don't have to lie about where they have been or where they are going. Yet life in prison isn't all a 'bed of roses'. Bullying can take place, ganging up and making life difficult for people who don't fit in or who won't do someone a favour, can make for an uncomfortable time. But it's better than being raped or used as a punch bag!

For the woman caught in the cycle of drug abuse, criminality and prison, she knows the rules of the road better than some of those upheld by society. I've asked many women in the past 'how are you?' and got the honest reply 's**t!' The 'etiquette of the road' doesn't demand a polite response, one flowered with ambiguity and a feigned smile. For some, my polite enquiry is a waste of time, space and energy. She just wants to 'crack-on' and in some cases literally head towards the 'crack-house', so has no time for small talk. What's the point? She doesn't aim to be rude, but neither does she care if it's interpreted that way. More than likely she's oblivious to how I feel about the encounter, and my feelings are irrelevant. If she hears me, knows me, or likes me, she may reply with a short 'alright', but if I offer to help I can get a qualified 'no, I'm alright', and without missing a beat she's moved on out of hearing range. I've stood alongside other Through The Gate staff as a woman has brushed by totally ignoring my greeting. 'How rude,' is the assessment of my colleague. I think to myself, 'Yup, in my world but not necessarily in hers.'

Addiction is all consuming. It occupies every conscious thought. It drives the mind and body to crave without distraction. Addiction possesses the person like a parasite entering a 'body' which it soon eats away at and destroys. No pleasantries are going to distract an addict from their journey to fulfil their ambition. Their rules are ones designed to make sure their target for the day is reached – whether they must lie, steal, con, abuse themselves or others to succeed. 'On't road' is a different 'world' to the one I prefer to operate in, but if I choose to engage with some of the women coming out of prison, then I must learn to accept some of these women have a different set of rules and etiquette, and I can't presume they are going to fit into my expectations.

Reflection

If you were . . .

. . . just released from prison – what would be the first thing you would look for or go to?

. . . supporting someone whose focus meant their communication with you was blunt – how would this make you feel and how would you manage it?

9

Asked out –
'Will you walk with me?'

EDITORIAL: to highlight the importance of a non-judgemental attitude when supporting people released from prison.

Aim: to acknowledge people can resettle positively from prison.

I'm walking down the corridor once again, heading towards the holding cell in the prison reception/departure area. The closer I get the noisier it becomes, and I start to brace myself for the encounter. I'm expecting the usual 'Who are you?' or being blanked as though only I can see myself in the room. I'm pleasantly surprised to see a face I know smiling at me as I enter. After a friendly greeting the woman asks if I'm going to walk her to the station. In fact, it's more of a demand.

We have walked down to the station before, a couple of times. However, this time she adds, 'but can we not go to the shop.' This is music to my ears! On numerous occasions I've either walked with her and waited outside the shop near to the prison, where she has purchased her preferred tipple, or seen her race ahead and come out with a bag full of 'goodies', often cans. She, like many women, has a developed pattern of celebrating release with a 'drink'. It's amazing how quickly it can have an effect. Within a few minutes the chatter can get louder, and the nature of the conversation can become more explicit or aggressive. The regulars know what they are doing and are usually not going to be persuaded to resist the temptation. If I debate the merits of their actions too long, then I'm running the risk of confrontation. I have some colleagues who believe I have special powers, which when deployed can make the most determined of alcohol seekers powerless in their quest to get intoxicated. I am such a let-down to some people. Of course, I do have super-powers, one of them is being 'non-judgmental', and I do wish more people had this one. When I deploy this one, it's amazing what results are produced. It is exactly because I'm non-judgemental that many women will engage with me and the very reason this woman did.

To access the shop, we must cross the road. However, we can get to the station without crossing the road at this point. Crossing over is significant – it's a wilful act. As is deciding not to, especially when it's normally the person's routine. This woman was making a conscious decision not to purchase and consume alcohol. Her motivation was later explained: she wanted to get to Probation sober. She wasn't promising abstinence, but her track record was of not usually making it to her first appointment and subsequently being recalled. Often, it's one simple decision at a time. Her action brought a 'warm feeling' of success, not of having consumed a large amount of vodka, I don't think the 'warm feeling' was down to alcohol! I'm not sure I've seen her since.

There are many women I don't see again. We walk together, wait a while on the station platform and I wave as she departs. And that's it, gone. There was a woman I saw recently at the prison, in the visitors' centre. She was someone I recognised from many years ago. I remember having a few conversations with her way back. We got talking and it turned out she was back visiting as a worker for a project. What surprised me was how many years ago it was, when she was last in as a prisoner. She was one of those regulars who was no longer a regular! In fact, I've seen her a couple of times now in her professional capacity, and she is fast becoming a regular of a very different sort. It's easy to forget we haven't seen someone, until we see them again.

Reflection

If you were . . .

. . . often in prison – what sort of support would you need to resettle positively back into the community?

. . . supporting a prison regular who says that this time their resettling back into the community will be different – how will you respond?

10

The 'F' Word …

EDITORIAL: to highlight how some women perceive themselves.

Aim: to encourage a sensitive approach to people who view themselves as failures.

'Failure', have you ever heard someone say, 'Failure doesn't exist'? I have, and it does my head in! They may go on to say how we shouldn't use the word 'failure', almost as if it's an expletive, but rather skirt around it by suggesting we restructure our sentences and use words like 'difficulties' or 'setbacks' and 'slip-ups'. I get that they are desperately trying not to label people as failures as this can sound harsh or even terminal. Yet to have 'failed' and know 'failure' is a reality. In my end-of-school exams, I got a 'U' in French – 'unclassified' or 'ungraded', which meant I had failed to achieve a grade – of any sort! However you wish to dress it up, I had failed. It wasn't a slip-up – I failed to achieve a grade and I believed at the time that I was a failure at French. In fact I failed in English comprehension too, getting an 'F' two years later. I never went back to French; I never resat the exam, and accepted the likelihood that I wasn't to become a fluent French speaker. And guess what – I'm not!

In this case I knew when to quit and what the reality of the situation was. However, where English comprehension is concerned, I never resat my English exams, but it didn't stop me from becoming an author – forty years later.

I have walked to the station with a few women who have described themselves as 'failures' and who am I to argue, so I listen. In one case my silence allowed space and time for the woman to reflect and suggest that she had failed rather than be a failure. The fact that I'm walking again with someone I had walked with previously makes it difficult for them to view themselves as a success. Their attempt to resettle permanently in the community ended in failure. Over the years they have had their children taken from their care and been adopted, they have lost contact with their family, they have had several attempts to detoxify from non-prescribed medication end in not only a return to drugs but an increased usage, they have been unable to maintain relationships or accommodation. Viewing themselves alongside others, some conclude they are failures.

I don't endorse the concept that the person I'm journeying alongside is a 'total failure', but I accept this can be their reading of their life at that moment. I must be careful that I don't appear to be in denial or minimising the gravity of the situation. If I debate the terminology, I run the risk of being another person who says they are wrong, another person criticising them and perhaps not giving them space to express how they feel. There is a time and a place to challenge the concept of failure and an art to doing it. I always try to drop into conversation something positive about the person I'm engaging with but I'm careful in my timing. Sometimes it is important we hold back from being 'politically' or 'socially' or 'intellectually' correct. I have a plea to those 'upbeat', 'it's not as bad as it looks' people. Stop for a moment before you say to someone that they haven't failed, or they are wrong to view themselves as a failure — when they have lost their children, family, friends, home, belongings, money, career, religion, health, self-esteem and hope! Please, just listen and nod and wait for the right time to put forward a different perspective.

Saying something positive to someone who is presenting as very low can take a bit of thought. The opposite to failure is success and I have come to redefine what success may look like for someone who is well known to the prison. I tend to measure success against previous experiences. If a person didn't engage before but has this time — that's success. If the person didn't get to the station sober previously but has this time — that too is success. Without being patronising, I try to highlight these small positive steps. Maybe this time they'll get to their appointments. And who knows what will happen in the future, sometimes the journey to achievement is a long one — in my case forty years to become an author from failing my English exams!

Reflection

If you were . . .

. . . someone who viewed yourself as a failure — would you want anyone disagreeing with you?

. . . working with someone who perceives themselves as a failure, but you are also struggling in that area — how would you support them?

11

'Oh my God ...'

EDITORIAL: to highlight the importance of finding an interest a prisoner can carry on in the community.

Aim: to encourage prison-based activities and departments to develop skills, interests or hobbies that prisoners can continue with in the community.

'I was so worried she was dead.' I've heard this a few times over the years when I've phoned a parent to let them know where their daughter is. It has also been followed by them saying how glad they are that their daughter is safe, as they were extremely worried about her because she hadn't been in contact for a long time. However, a few have gone on to ask me to let her know that, whilst they are pleased they have heard from her, they still cannot put her up once she is released. I had one mum tell me how in fear their other children are when their daughter turns up and very often causes mayhem.

'Oh my God' isn't often used in my presence solely as an expletive, but rather as an adjective, an expression of relief. In the context above, there was much relief! Sometimes it's uttered in expectation, especially when I've told someone I have something specific to tell them, but sometimes it's shouted out. Sharing good and bad news can often draw this response. I've been in the reception area when a woman has been told she has accommodation already in place and there is someone outside waiting to take her by taxi to her destination. I've even seen tears at the relief. Yet I've also been there when a woman has been told that the support she was expecting outside hasn't materialised and she must get herself to somewhere unfamiliar and hope something can be sorted out when she arrives. Her response may be, 'Oh my God, what do they expect me to do? I don't know where I'm going, I've got no money and I'm going to be late.' She may then go on to swear, panic and say how let down she feels, particularly at such short notice. Some see incidents like this as a 'kick in the teeth', especially as she has agreed to comply, something she doesn't normally do.

However, for some women 'Oh my God' is a declaration of faith. It has been said that people in prison can get the gym bug, the education bug or get God. Physical training, education development and faith are all encouraged in prison, within certain parameters, but some people can go over the top. Some prisoners rediscover their childhood or parents' faith, taking time to learn more about it or take it a little more seriously. Sometimes we try to curb their enthusiasm, especially when they want to convert their cell mate, others on the wing and just about anyone else they meet. This can be unhelpful! Not everyone is, of course, genuine about their engagement, and chaplaincy activities, the gym and education can be used as places to trade contraband.

Finding an interest in prison – like exercise, studying and faith – can be helpful when people leave prison. When I'm walking down to the station with someone I will often ask if they know what they are going to do with their time now they are out. It's not uncommon for me to hear someone say that they want to become a counsellor and do some studying or finish off some distance-learning course. Some can't wait to get down the gym or even go swimming if they can afford it. Knowing I'm a chaplain, some will talk about going back to their 'Temple' – often used to describe various places of worship – or how they plan to attend church 'this Sunday'. Very often they will know where their nearest building or group is. However, we often get a request in chaplaincy to link someone with a faith community outside. Keeping prisoners in touch with their interests is extremely valuable, as often it is part of their culture or lifestyle, something comforting and familiar, and can assist in their introduction back into the community. I always encourage the person I'm with to carry on with whatever they are interested in, if it's healthy and even if it's a faith I personally don't follow, lifting weights or studying number theory!

Reflection

If you were . . .

. . . just coming out of prison – what activity would you be looking to pick up again?

. . . advising someone about embarking upon an activity – how would you go about identifying an appropriate one?

12

Where are they now?

EDITORIAL: to highlight how some people come out of prison and vanish, deliberately or otherwise.

Aim: to encourage services, family members and friends to keep in touch with people after they come out of prison when appropriate; and how important it is.

I've been asked a couple of times, by a woman standing in front of me in the holding cell, if I remember the woman she was with last time because that woman is now dead. Sadly, hearing that a prisoner you have known has died, especially if it's a drug-related death, is no longer the shock it once was. Naturally there are some prisoners you know better than others and hearing of their demise can be upsetting. Occasionally you hear that they died only a few hours after their release and the conjecture amongst the women is that either it was a bad batch or her body wasn't used to the strength, especially if she had partially detoxed inside. For the regulars, you always hope that this time they will leave and get themselves 'sorted', 'clean'. When you don't see them for a while, you hope the next news is good news but, unfortunately, too many times it's not.

There are women who promise to keep in touch with 'friends' they've made inside. But after a couple of letters, they disappear. It is common for people who have left prison after only one sentence to want to forget all about their experience. Some have families who will certainly cover for them when they are inside so that, when they are back in circulation, the story that they have been working away is the one everyone knows about. What brings someone to prison can be so shameful for them that they hope no one ever finds out. Some people change their name because of their past or for the sake of their children who, if it were known what their mum has done in the past, could cause them problems. They work hard at blending back into the community or putting down roots in a new one. Moving to escape an 'ex' or start afresh is a common story and sometimes there is a lot of truth in it. Or they tell how they have relocated to begin a new job, only for it to not work out. I've known a few women who, some years after leaving, have stable relationships, found work, and had children. They could be the person next door or over the road and you just don't know, and why should you? Most people who have been in prison are not 'mass murderers' waiting to drink your blood the moment your back is turned! For whatever reason, they have found themselves convicted, imprisoned and released.

Of course, many of us like a 'feel good' story: someone who has overcome adversity, had a bad start in life, been to the darkest of places and now, with hard work and good support, have seen their lives turned around and are now taking an active role in the community and making a difference where they are. There are those stories out there, but we don't get to hear many of them because people just want to get on with their lives, without people staring at them or feeling obliged to explain themselves. However, I know two people who have written books and they are superb – both the people and the books. They are humble, honest and genuinely reformed women; fantastic examples of how lives can be turned around. Both attribute their new lives to their faith, and both have been living this new life for many years, standing the test of time.

Where are those I've walked to the station with now? I hope they are safe, well, getting on with life, living it to the full, but I don't know, nor do I have to. However, the policy makers, budget setters and politicians need to know, to justify expenditure or policies. Case managers in the community may need to know in order to keep the community safe as well as the ex-prisoner. Hopefully, the families know where their partners, daughters, sisters and mums are, but this is not always the case. Some come out of prison and are lost – they vanish, sometimes never to reappear. Now I've got to go and read a good-news story of someone who has found true freedom, a new life, joy and happiness; and maybe I'll sleep tonight.

Reflection

If you were . . .

. . . going 'home' after leaving prison – how would you feel about telling people where you had been or why you were there?

. . . working with someone who has come out of prison – do you think it is important that the community know where they have been?

Be Free

Be free to be you,

Be free to be safe,

Be free to dream,

Be free to laugh,

Be free to cry,

Be free to succeed,

Be free to fail,

Be free to take your time,

Be free to run,

Be free to rest,

Be free to speak,

Be free to listen,

Be free to learn,

Be free to forget,

Be free to stop,

Be free to go again.

Simeon Sturney

Acknowledgements

I was inspired to write this booklet when taking part in the Alumni Programme with The Butler Trust and am grateful to the support and encouragement from Helen and Andrew. I am always mindful of the support I have been given by colleagues, including dedicated volunteers who have assisted me with the Through The Gate support we offer. Huge thanks also go to the women I walk alongside, who have enlightened me and taught me so much. Once again I must thank the publishers Malcolm Down and Sarah Grace for their technical input and expertise, very much appreciated. Finally, special thanks go to my family and friends who have once again journeyed with me as I've discussed the manuscript and benefited from their insight and encouragement.